韓國民俗村

Korean Folk Village

■ 韓國民俗村 KOREAN FOLK VILLAGE

민속촌 세운 뜻 : 우리 겨레는 아름다운 금수강산인 이 땅위에서 유구한 역사를 누려오는 동안 하나의 특유한 민족성과 독창적인 민속문화를 이룩하였읍니다.

그러므로 이것을 보존하고 전승하여 발전시켜 나아가는 것은 우리들의 소중한 의무라 하겠읍니다. 따라서 우리는 이곳을 한국의 전통문화와 고유한 전래의 풍속을 배울 수 있는 교실이자 박물관으로, 그리고 외국인까지도 우리 겨레의 조상 대대로 전해오는 생활풍속의 옛 모습과 멋을 느낄 수 있는 전시장으로서 이 민속촌을 세우게 된 것입니다. 30만 여평의 대지위에 250여채의 집들이 모두 우리 고유의 건축양식이요. 또 각지방의 가옥 구조를 살필 수 있는 것이므로 마치 그 옛날 왕조시대의 한 고을을 그대로 제현시켜 놓은 것임을 느낄수 있는 곳입니다. 또 이곳에서는 옛 조상들의 슬기와 솜씨를 볼 수 있는 민속공예품과 각종 가구들이 있어 지난 시대의 숨소리 마져 들을 수 있을 것입니다.   그러므로 이 민속촌은 우리 모두의 것입니다. 우리 다 같이 사랑과 보호로 길이 후손들에게 물려줄 수 있도록 아끼고 키워 주시기 바랍니다.

A home for the true Korean heritage our ancestors created a unique national character and culture on this beautiful pen in sula, and they took care to preserve them through a long history. It is our noble duty to cherish and develop our heritage for succeeding generations.

With this mission in mind. We have established the Korean Folk village as a museum and a learning center for traditional Korean culture so that we and foreigners may feel and experience the Korean way of life in all authentic atmosphere.

The village, on an area of 300,000 pyong, is a replice of a typical 19th century Korean village with more than 250 houses and buildings representing all parts of area. The village structures, used for various functions, feature traditional furniture and products demonstrating the brilliance and elegance of our ancestors.

The Korean Folk village is for all of us. We, the staff of the village will do our best to make it worthy of your visit.

目　　次
Contents

民 俗 村 概 觀・An Outline of the Korean Folk Village

觀 覽 案 內・A Tour Guide・・・2

三 　 　 門・Three Passage Gate・・・・・・・・・・・・・・・・・・・・・・・・・・・・・・・・・・・・4

孝 子 門・Monument For A Dutiful Son・・・・・・・・・・・・・・・・・・・・・・・5

연 자 방 아・Yon Ja Pang-A (Millstone)・・・・・・・・・・・・・・・・・・・・・・6

陶 磁 器・Ceramic Kiln・・8

南 部 地 方 農 家・Farmer's House in the Southern Part・・・버들공방 Willow Ware・・・・・・・・・・・10

南 部 地 方 小 農 家・Peasan'ts House in the Southern Part・・・싸리공방 Lespedeza Ware・・・・・・・12

北 部 地 方 民 家・Farmer's House in the Northern Part・・・・・・・・・・・・・・・・・・・・・・・・・・・14

南 部 地 方 大 家・Manor House in the Southern Part・・・・・・혼례 (婚禮) Wedding・・・・・・・・15

南 部 地 方 中 農 家・Middle-class Farmer's House in the・・・죽공방 (竹工房) Bambooware・・・18
　　　　　　　　　　　　Southern Part

藥 　 房・Chinese Herb Shop・・・・・・・・・・・・・・・・・・・・・・・・・・・・・・・・・・・・・・・20

南 部 地 方 農 家・Former's House in the Southern Part・・・완초공예 Rushware・・・・・・・・・・22

南 部 地 方 小 農 家・Peasant's House in the Southern Part・・・・・・・・・・・・・・・・・・・・・・・・・24

中 部 地 方 農 家・Farmer's House in the Midland・・・・・・・・・명주길쌈 Silk Weaving・・・・・25

金 連 寺・Keumnyonsa Temple・・・・・・・・・・・・・・・・・・・・・・・・・・・・・・・・・・・28

官 　 衛・Provincial Governor's Office・・・・・・・・・・・・・・・・・・・・・・・・・30

南 部 地 方 民 家・House in the Southern Part・・・・・・・・・・・・점술 (卜術) Shaman Devination・・・・32

南 部 地 方 民 家・House in the Southern Part・・・・・・・・・・・・・・・・・・・・・・・・・・・・・・・34

中 部 地 方 民 家・Farmer's House in the Midland・・・・・・・・・・・・・・・・・・・・・・・・・・・35

中 部 地 方 班 家・Midland Mansion・・・・・・・・・・・・・・・・・・・・・・・・・・・・・・・・・・・36

北 部 地 方 民 家・Farmer's House in the Northern Part・・・닥종이제조 Mulberry Paper Manufacturing・・・40

市 　 場・Market Place・・・42

물 레 방 아 (水車)・Water-mill・・・・・・・・・・・・・・・・・・・・・・・・・・・・・・・・・・・・・・・44

中 部 地 方 民 家・Farmer's House in the Midland・・・・・・・・・・・엿집 Gluten Candy・・・・・・46

濟 州 島 民 家・Cheju Houses・・・・・・・・・・・・・・・・・・・・・・・・・・・・・・・・・・・・・48

南 海 沿 岸 民 家・Seaside House in the Southern Part・・・・・・・・・・・・・・・・・・・・・・50

鬱 陵 島 民 家・Ulleung Houses・・・・・・・・・・・・・・・・・・・・・・・・・・・・・・・・・・・51

硏 經 書 院・Private School・・・・・・・・・・・・・・・・・・・・・・・・・・・・・・・・・・・・・・54

公 演 場・Performing Arena・・・・・・・・・農樂 (널뛰기) Farmer's Music-And-Dance Seesawing・・・56

中 部 地 方 民 家・Farmer's House in the Midland・・・・・・・・・・・・・・・・・・・・・・・・・・・53

南 部 地 方 民 家・Farmer's House in the Southern Part・・・書堂 Private School・・・・・・57

南 部 地 方 民 家・Farmer's House in the Southern Part・・・草工藝 Rushware・・・・・・・・60

中 部 地 方 民 家・Farmer's House in the Midland・・・・・・・・・・・・・・・・・・・・・・・・・・61

南 部 地 方 大 家・Big House in the Southern Part・・・・・・・・・・・・・・・・・・・・・・・・・62

南 部 地 方 民 家・Farmer's House in the Southern Part・・・담뱃대工房 Tobacco Pipe Maker's Workshop・・・64

中 部 地 方 民 家・Farmer's House in the Midland・・・・・・・・・・・・・・・・・・・・・・・・・66

中 部 地 方 民 家・Farmer's House in the Midland・・・・・・・・・・・・・・・・・・・・・・・・・67

대 장 간 (冶匠間)・Black smith's Workshop・・・・・・・・・・・・・・・・・・・・・・・・・・・68

農 機 具 展 示 場・Showroom for Farming Tools・・・・・・・・・・・・・・・・・・・・・・70

鍮 器 工 房・Brassware Maker's workshop・・・・・・・・・・・・・・・・・・・・・・71

삼　　문(三門)
THREE-PASSAGE GATE

　삼문(三門)에는 평삼문, 솟을삼문, 누삼문등이 있으며, 궁궐 및 공청(관아, 향교), 서원등의 정면에 있는 문이다.
　이곳의 평삼문(平三門)은 전시지역과 상가지역을 구분하기 위하여 세운 건물이다.

　In the kinds of the Three-Passage Gates there are the flat ones, the lofty ones, and the towered ones that used to stand in front of the castles, the public halls (the Government Offices or the Country Institutes), and the Confucian Schools.
　The above Flat Three-Passage Gate is a structure set up to divide our village into two areas-the area available and the exhibition area.

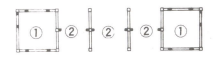

① 방(room)
② 대문(gate)

효 자 문 (孝子門)
MONUMENT FOR ADUTIFULSON

효자 이덕규(李德圭. 1850〜1900) 의 효행을 기념한 정문(旌門)이다. 「효자문」(孝子門) 또는 「정여」(旌閭) 라고도 하며 사람의 통행이 많은 위치에 세워진다. 이문은 1904년에 세워졌던 것인데 원형대로 옮겨진 것이다. 효자나 열녀의 정문은 유서있는 마을어귀에서 흔히 볼 수 있는 기념물이다.

This is the monument erected in 1904 is memory of Yi Togkyu, man of filial piety. Its location was on a crossroad for everybody to look at it. The monument has been removed from there to here in its origieal form.

연자방아(**YONJA PANG-A**) MILL STONE

초정과 같이 짚을 이어 짓되 9개의 기둥을 원형으로 돌려 세워, 지붕도 둥글게 끊어 마무리한 초정 형식이다.

연자매는 그 돌바탕이 둥글고 그것을 끌며 도는 소가 둥글게 돌아가므로 그 기능에 맞도록 집이 지어진다.

연자매는 가축의 힘을 이용하는 도정(搗精) 기구로서, 종래 우리 농촌에서 널리 사용되어 왔다.

This is the reproduction the 19th century millstone as found in Hwasong and Namyang districts, Kyonggi-do. It is under the thatched roof propped by 9posts positioned in a circle. As the ox toes round, the roundshaped millstone rolls circling. The millstone was the most popular mill among Korean farmers in the past.

초정(草亭) 내부
The inside of the thatched roof pavilion
연자매
Millstone

④ 도자기가마(陶窯) CERAMIC KILN

우리나라의 도자기라고 하면 고려청자와 이조의 백자 분청사기로 유명하다. 도자기는 한마디로 흙과 불로서 이루어지는 변화무궁한 공예품이다.

흙은 살이 되고 잿물(灰汁)은 반들거리는 유약(釉藥)이 된다. 가마의 설비는 흙을 빚어 그릇을 성형(成形)하고 다듬고, 말리는 작업장과 구어내는 가마로 구성된다. 여기에 쓰이는 자토(磁土)는 특수한 백점토(白粘土)로서 불순물을 가려내고 수비(水飛)해서 앙금을 얻어내어 곱게 이겨서 사용하게 된다. 흙반죽을 물레위에 얹고 발로 물레를 차 돌리면서 두손으로 그릇을 빚어 올

린다. 성형이 되면 말려서 일단 가마에 재여 초벌구이(800℃)하고 단단해진 기벽(器壁)에 무늬를 새기거나 그린다음 약통물에 담가서 유약을 바르고, 다시 가마에 재어 재벌구이(1300℃)하면 그릇이 완성된다.

Representative of Korean pottery are Koryo celadon and Yi dynasty white ceramics. Celadon and ceramics are products of fire and clay and glaze. The production process involves the kneading into dough of clay, the formation of vessel bases and baking. First, the material, white clay, is purified by the elimination of impurities from it and formed into vessel bases on a potter's wheel. The vessel bases are then baked in 800 degree C. heat before designs are painted or engraved on their surface, when the painting or engraving is done glaze is applied on their surface before the bases are baked for the second time, this time in 1,300 degree C. heat. The outcome is pottery.

상감작업
Work of inlying inlaying

독짓는 모습
A posture forming a jar

도자기 가마와 작품
A ceramic kiln with the pottery products

⑤ 남부지방농가 南部地方農家
FARMER'S HOUSE IN THE SOUTHERN PART

48평 (160.23M²)　19세기경　양식
48PYONG OR 160.23M²　STYLE OF 19th CENTURY

안채와 바깥채 두 채가 모두 일자형이며 앞뒤에 평행으로 배치된 형식이다. 규모는 호남지방의 견실한 중농가에 속하며 안채에는 방과 마루공간이 많아 개방성을 띠었다. 바깥채에는 광이 많으며 사랑방과 머슴방이 달려있다.

This is the reproduction of a 19th century middle-class farmer's house as found in Anp'yongri, Changsongkun, Chollanam-do. The straight-line inner wing and the straingt-line outer wing stand paralled to each other. The scale of the house shows that the house belonged to a middle-class farmer with solid income. The number of rooms, four in all, and the wooden-floor veranda installed along the front and one side of the wing denotes, among others, the openness of the house. The outer wing consists of a drawing-room, a servant's room, a cowshed, three store rooms, and the gate.

버들공방
Willow WARE

 알갱이로 털어낸 곡식이나 도정한 곡식을 담아 까불러서 죽정이와 껍질, 검부래기 따위를 날려 보내는 제구. 지역에 따라 버들가지로 만들기도 하고 얇게 뜬 대올로 엮기도 하는데 그 모양에도 차이가 있다.

 A winnowing fan is an instrumen to have the blasted ears, chaff or remnants or dry grass or leaves blown off by tossing the winnowing fan, after some of shaken off or milled grain or kernel is put in the fan. According to the area this winnowing fan is woven and made of pussy willows or the thin detached bamboo plys in a different shape.

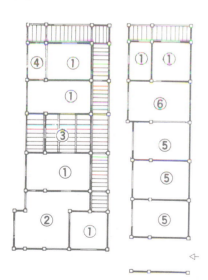

① 방 (room)
② 부엌 (kitchen)
③ 마루 (Wooden floor)
④ 골방 (back room)
⑤ 광 (store room)
⑥ 외양간 (cowshed)

11

⑥ 남부지방소농가 南部地方小農家

FARMER'S HOUSE IN THE SOUTHERN PART

20평 (66.87M²)   **19세기경 양식**
20PYONG OR 66.87M²   STYLE OF 19th CENTURY

3칸을 겨우 넘는 일자형의 소 농가 형식이다. 사랑채가 따로 없고 대청 건너편방이 사랑방이며 따라서 안쪽으로는 벽이 막혀 있다. 마루 공간이 고루 안배되어 남쪽지방 농가 특유의 개방성과 기능성을 지니고 있다.

This is the reproduction of a 19th century peasant's house as found in Changanri, Changsongkun, Chollanam-do. There is only one straight-line wing to this house. The wooden-floor room is between the inner and the minor rooms. The existence of two wooden-floor veranda in front of the inner room and at the side of the minor room denotes the openness characteristic of farmer's houses in this part of Korea.

① 방(room)
② 부엌(kichen)
③ 마루(wooden floow)

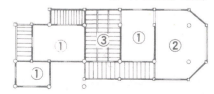

싸리공방
Lespedeza WARE

우리나라 어느곳의 야산에서 자생
하는 다년생 나무로써 먼 옛날부터 싸
리를 이용하여 생활에 필요한 기물을
만들어 사용되어 왔다.

싸리는 일년중 중복부터 말복까지
의 싸리를 제일좋은 질로 껍질을 벗
겨 사용하였고, 가을, 겨울의 싸리는
삶아 껍질을 벗겨 사용하여 번거스러
운 작업을 하였다.

대개 기물을 만들때는 형태를 굵은
살로 형을 짜면서 가는살로 연결하여
짠다.

흔히 제품으로는 용수, 채반, 광주
리, 반지고리, 고리, 다래끼 등의 주
방용기, 생활용기. 농기구등이 있다.

On any hills in Korea a lespedeza
grows wild as a perennial plant, so it
has been in use to make necessary
utensils of living from old times.

From the middle period of dog days
to the last of the dog days every year
one lespedeza has been in use as the best
quality by taking off the bark from
it, and the other lespedeza has been in
use, by taking off the bark from it
after being boiled, with difficult work
in fall and in winter.

This lespedeza ware is woven to be
connected with the thin ribs, and to
form ware with the thick ribs, when
being made.

In the wares there are a rice-wine
strainer, a wicker tray, a round basket,
a sewing-box, a wicker trunk, and a
basket with a small opening, for kitchen
utensils, tools of living, farm implements, and etc.

⑦ 북부지방민가 北部地方民家
FARMER'S HOUSE IN THE NORTHERN PART

28. 78평 (102. 07M²)   **19세기경 양식**
28. 78PYONG OR 102. 07M²   STYLE OF 19th CENTURY

일곱채의 집이 널리 산개(散開) 되어 있는 특이한 민가의 형식이다. 안채와 문간채, 사랑채, 광채의 4동을 기본으로해서 튼 □자형으로 배치하였다. 전반적으로 키가 낮고 칸사리가 비교적 좁아 동수에 비례한 평수는 적은것이 특징이다. 문간채와 사랑채 뒤에 따로 변소가 있다.

This reproduction which consists of

seven detached wings is a typical 19th century farmer's house as found in Anju. P'yongannam-do. The inner wing, the outer or gate wing, the drawing-room wing, and the store wing are the four main wings, the lay-out of which modelled itself upon the letter '□' with four open corners. The number of the wings is impressive, but their actual measurements are not very big because of the narrow breadth between the

props. The toilet is located behind the drawing-room wing.

① 방 (room)
② 부엌 (kichen)
③ 마루 (wooden-floor)
④ 광 (store-room)
⑤ 헛간 (bara)
⑥ 외양간 (cowshed)
⑦ 변 소 (toilet)

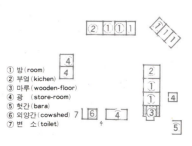

⑨ 남부지방대가 南部地方大家
MANOR HOUSE IN THE SOUTHERN PART

82. 58평 (266M²)   **19세기경 양식**
82.58PYONG OR 266M²   STYLE OF 19th CENTURY

ㄷ자형의 안채와 ㄱ자형의 사랑채에 일자형 (一字形)의 광채와 문간채 등 4동의 집이 튼 □자형으로 구성된 형식이며 전라도 무안에서 옮겨 온 고가이다. 전반적으로 마루와 툇마루, 누마루가 고루 배설되어 있으며 안채와 사랑채의 온돌, 마루가 차지 하는 면적의 크기는 서로 비슷한 비례이다. 넓고 시원하며 또 아기자기한 공간 구성은 여유있는 문화생활의 영위를 가능케 하는 것이다.

This is the reproduction of a 19th century mansion as found in Muan district, Chollanam-do. The inner wing shaped like the letter 'ㄷ', the drawing-room wing shaped like the letter 'ㄱ', the straight-line store wing, and the straight-line gate wing are so positioned as to make the form of the letter 'ㅁ'.

The first two wings have all the necessary items like the wooden-floor room, wooden-floor veranda, and riased wooden-floor room. The space of the floor-rooms is as large as that of the rooms. On the whole, the spaciousness of the house enabled the family with money and leisure to enjoy their cultural life.

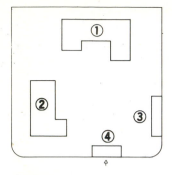

① 안채 (inner wing)
② 사랑채 (drawing-room wing)
③ 광채 (Store wing)
④ 대문간 (gate wing)

안채
INNER WING

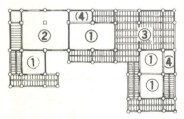

① 방 (room)
② 부엌 (kitchen)
③ 대청 (wooden floor-hall)
④ 마루 (wooden floor)

사랑채
DRAWING ROOM WING

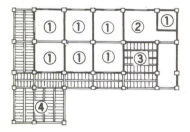

① 방 (room)
② 대청 (wooden floor-hall)
③ 누마루 (raised wooden-floor)
④ 골방 (back room)

혼례(婚禮) WEDLING

중매에 의하여 배우자가 선택되면 결
혼 당사자는 얼굴도 보지 못한채 궁합,
사주, 택일을 정하여 혼례를 갖춘다.

신부는 얼굴에 연지 곤지를 바르고 원
삼 쪽두리에 신랑을 맞는다.

신랑은 사모관대 의장에 말을 타고
신부의 집으로 와서 혼례행사를 치른다.

When a wedding had been ar-
ranged between a go-between and
the parents of the bride and bridegroom-to-be, an auspicious date
was selected for the wedding.
The wedding would start with
the bridegroom-to-be riding a horse
to the house of the bride-to-be
to hold an initial wedding rite
called "chorye."

The bridegroom-to-be was accompanied by his father or grand-
father.   An entourage consisting
of gift-bearers, servants and friends
also accompanied him.   After the
procession reached the bride-to-
be's house the entourage all returned home leaving the groom to
spend his first night with his bride
at the latter house. The following
day the bridegroom returned
home with his bride in a ritual
process called "chohaeng."   The
newly wed couple spent three days
at the groom's house before they
again visited the house of the
bride where they spent three more
days. With his over, the couple
returned to the groom's house to
begin a normal married life.

⑩ 남부지방중농가 南部地方中農家   32. 42평 (107. 19M²) 19세기경   양식
MIDDLE-CLASS FARMER'S HOUSE IN THE SOUTHERN PART 32. 42PYONG OR 107. 19M² STYLE OF 19th CENTURY

안채와 사랑채가 모두 일자형이며 앞 뒤 평행으로 배치 되었다. 유래있는 시골 선비집으로 사랑채에 4칸 대청과 두개의 큰 방을 갖추었으며 안채에는 찬간과 감실(사당)을 갖추었다.

This is the reproduction of a 19th century house as found in Changanri, Changsongkun, Cholla-nam-do. The house consists of the inner and outer straight-line wings which are positioned parallel to each other. The house having belonged to a noted country scholar, its drawing-room wing (the outer wing) has a big hall with fourfold props and two large rooms. The inner wing is furnished with, among others, a pantry and a family shrine.

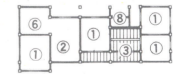

① 방 (room)
② 부엌 (kitchen)
③ 마루 (wooden-floor)
④ 대청 (wooden-floor hall)
⑤ 광 (store-room)
⑥ 찬간 (pantry)
⑦ 골방 (back room)
⑧ 사당 (tamily shrine)

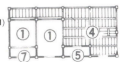

죽 공 예 Bamboo WARE

죽물(竹物)—죽세공(竹細工)하면 담양(潭陽)이라고 할만큼 죽물의 고장은 호남지방이다. 죽세공의 극치는 채상(彩箱)이다. 이는 대나무 표피(表皮)부분을 엷고 가늘게 쪼개어 고리(箱子)를 짜는 것인데 그 대올에다 여러 색깔로 염색해 비단같은 무늬를 놓기 때문에 채상이라 일컫는 것이다. 이 편죽법(編竹法)에 의하여 피죽궤(皮竹櫃), 반짓고리, 방갓, 삿갓등을 만들기도 한다. 근자에는 핸드백 종류도 만든다. 부채,

특히, 합죽선(合竹扇)은 한국 죽세 공예의 독특한 일면이며, 참빗이나 발(簾)도 마찬가지다. 그리고 목공제품에 대쪽을 붙이는 예가 적지 않으며 필통, 찬합, 고비등의 소품에 죽제(竹製)의 정교한 물건이 있다. 그밖에도 갓의 양태와 대열개미도 특수한 제품이고, 산백죽(山白竹)으로는 조리를 만들고 시누대(箭竹)로는 화살을 만든다.

Bambooware is a speciality of Tamyang in south Choila province. Boxes made of thin stripes of bamboo dyed in many colors are especially famous for their beauty. Bambooware of Tamyang also includes woven work-baskets, hats, screens and fans.

⑪ 약 방
CHINESE HERB SHOP

30. 47평(101. 71M²) **19세기경 양식**
30. 47PYONG OR 101. 71M² STYLE OF 19th CENTURY

　재래의 한약국을 경영하던 중부지방 도회민가의 한 형식이다. 진찰실과 약방, 약재의 저장과 처리를 위한 방이 각각 기능 위주로 안배되고 일상적 생활공간은 위축된 경향을 보인다. 중인계층의 직업적 생활 공간을 짐작할 수 있는 가옥이다.

This is the reproduction of a 19th century urban Chinese herb shop as found in Kaesong, Kyonggi-do. The placement and size of the rooms show that every priority was given to the shop operation. More space is allocated to the consultation room, herb-room, and herb-storing room to the dwelling-rooms, This house shows what the place of a professional middle-class man was like.

① 방 (room)
② 부엌 (kitchen)
③ 마루 (wooden-floor)
④ 광 (store-room)
⑤ 헛간 (bara)
⑥ 약국 (herb-room)
⑦ 진찰실 (consaltation room)
⑧ 약재고 (herb-storing room)

⑫ 남부지방농가 南部地方農家
FARMER'S HOUSE IN THE SOUTHERN PART

31.09평(105.75M²)
31.09PYONG OR 105.75M²

19세기경 양식
STYLE OF 19th CENTURY

남부지방의 농가로서는 매우 드물게 ㄱ자형(字型)으로 안채를 꾸민 형식이다. 대소 3동이 여유있게 산개되었으며 마루와 같은 남부적 공간은 안채에만 한정되어 있다. 안부엌에 딸린 방이 작으며 대청이 뒷쪽으로 물려진 것은 특이한 형식이다.

This is the reproduction of a 19th century farmer's house as found in Kimhae district, Kyongsangnam-do. The inner wing is shaped like the letter 'ㄱ'; which is uncommon for a farmer's house in the southern part. Three wings constitute this farm house but only the inner wing has a wooden-floor room. It is noteworthy that the room next to the main kitchen is smaller than the others.

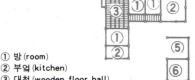

① 방 (room)
② 부엌 (kitchen)
③ 대청 (wooden floor hall)
④ 광 (store-room)
⑤ 헛간 (bara)
⑥ 변소 (toilet)

완초공예(莞草工藝)

RUSH WARE

왕골은 방동산이과에 속하는 일년
초로서 높이 90cm～150cm정도 자라며
그 줄기의 단면은 세모꼴이며 껍질은
매우 질기고 부드러워 자리나 방석,
바구니 따위를 짠다. 파종은 4월에
하는데 대게 물논(水畓)의 한 모퉁이
에 쓸만큼 심는다. 파종은 논바닥에
못자리처럼 이랑을 고르고 하되 재를
밑거름으로 한다. 싹이 자라면 6월
하순에 물논의 한쪽을 나직한 둑으로
막고 옮겨 심는데 오래된 벽토(壁土)
나 재(灰), 말똥따위로 거름을 주며
9월 하순에 베어 들인다. 베어 들인
왕골을 가는 새끼로 엮어서 이슬을 맞
히며 희게 바래서 쓴다. 유명한 강화
의 꽃돗자리도 왕골로 짜여지며 종래
민가에서 많이 쓰이던 왕골자리가 곧
이것으로 만들어 지는 것이다.

Rush is an annual plant attaining
a height of 90 to 150 centimeters.
Its stem is shaped like a triangle in
a cross-sectional view; and its skin
is very durable but soft, suitable
for seats, mats, and baskets.

The seeds are sown in Aprill
generally in one corner of a paddy
in a quanity which satisfies one
family's need. Ridges are erected
to sow the seeds like a rice seedbed.
The rush seedings are transplanted
to another corner of a paddy surrounded by a small dike to ward off
the water. Ashes are used as
fertilizer. The trans-plantation ta-
kes place late in June. Rush is
harvested late in september.

Rush is plaited like a screen with
a straw rope. It is cast away to
fade in dew before being used.
The famous colored mats of Kang-
hwa Island are made of rush. Also
made of rush are seats, a familler
household item. Rush mats are
not so intricate to weave, thick
but light, glossy and shapely. Today multi-colored baskets are woven with rush.

⑬ 남부지방소농가 南部地方小農家

PEASANT'S HOUSE IN THE SOUTHERN PART

8. 82평 (29. 16M²)
8. 82 PYONG OR 29. 16M²

19 세기경 양식
STYLE OF 19th CENTURY

두개의 방과 큰 부엌외양간을 갖춘 소농가의 형식이다. 안방과 윗방 사이에 마루나 토방이 없는 소규모의 이러한 농가형식이 매우 흔한것은 아니다. 그 구조는 내륙지방 가옥의 폐쇄성이나 경비절감과 같은 여건과 관련이 있어 보인다.

This is the reproduction of a 19th century peasant's house as found in Andong district, Kyong-sangbuk-do. The house consists of two rooms, a kitchen, and a cowshed and no more. There are no wooden-floor rooms and no earthen-floor verandas. Its structure denotes the closeness of inland house and the reduction of the building cost.

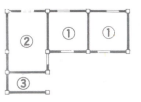

① 방 (room)
② 부엌 (kitchen)
③ 외양간 (cowshed)

⑭ 중부지방농가 中部地方農家
FARMER'S HOUSE IN THE MIDLAND

72. 08평 (238. 29M²) **19 세기경 양식**
72. 08 PYONG OR 238. 29 M² STYLE OF 19th CENTURY

안채와 사랑채의 두 ㄱ자형 집을 마주 배치한 중부지방 전형적 민가를 기본으로 하고 따로 하인들이 거처하는 행랑채와 방앗간, 마굿간 등 세 채의 집을 고루 갖춘 독농가이자 선비의 집이다. 매우 규모가 큰 초가집이다.

This is the reproduction of a typical 19th century midland farmer's house as found in Ichon district, Kyonggi-do. Two wings with the shape of letter 'ㄱ' stand facing each other. Attached to them is the haengrang wing for servants, a mill, and a stable. This can be said to have been the house of a diligent and prosperous farmer and scholar in Chinese classics who worked during the daytime and read at night or who worked on the farm on a fine day but read at home on a rainy day. It is a straw-thatched house thought the owner seems to have been rich enough to afford more than that.

① 방 (room)
② 부엌 (kichen)
③ 대청 (wooden-floor hall)
④ 광 (seore-room)
⑤ 헛간 (bara)
⑥ 외양간 (cpwshed)
⑦ 방아간 (mill)
⑧ 마구간 (stable)
⑨ 변소 (toilet)
⑩ 마루 (wooden- floor)

명주길쌈
SILK WEAVING

수직(手織)명주도 삼베, 모시와 같이 현대에는 귀한 옷감으로 여기게 되었다. 명주의 역사는 삼베와 마찬가지로 이미 삼한(三韓) 시대에서 시작 되었으며 누에치기에서 옷감이 되기까지 대개 농가 부업적 가내 수공업방식에 의해 생산되는 과정도 고금에 큰차이가 없다고 하겠다.

누에고치는 천연섬유로된 누에집이며, 이것을 여러개 동시에 끓는 물에 띄워서 실을 뽑는데, 고치가 10개면 거미줄보다 가는 10올의 섬유가 한올의 실로 뽑혀 나오게된다. 10올의 실은 보통 가는실이며 20개면 명주의 올이 굵어진다. 실을 얻은 후에 그것을 날고 매어서 틀에 올려 짜내기 까지의 과정은 무명이나 모시 삼베의 경우와 공통이다. 명주의 한재(升)는 실20올인데, 보름새(15새) 면 300올로 굵은 편이고 20새면 400올로서 발이 곱고 상등품이 된다.

Hand-woven silk is now rated as precious cloth like hemp and ramie cloth. All cloth woven by hand by the traditional method is generally becoming more expensive. Mainly because its production is extremely inactive and limited. Hand-woven, it is thick, durable, and trustworthy.

Silk dates back to the Samhan period, like hemp cloth. Silk is produced by farm families as a sideline as in the past through all its process, from silkworm raising to weaving.

Cocoons, source of natural fibre,

are set afloat on boiling water and threads are extracted. Ten piles of thread, as thin as a spider's, are obtainable from ten cocoons.

The process of silk weaving after obtaining the threads is the same as in the case of weaving hemp or ramie cloth.

무명길쌈
COTTON WEAVING

면(綿)을 한국어로는 무명 혹은 목(木)이라고 통칭한다. 더러 목면(木綿)이라고 쓰는 것은 수목(樹木)의 뜻과 구분하기 위한 복합어이다. 또 무명을 「목화(木花)」, 「면화(綿花)」라고 칭하기도 한다. 무명은 조선시대에 화폐와 같은 것이어서 나라에 바치는 쌀을 대신하였고, 관료들의 급료로 지불될 만큼 가치가 있었다. 한국에서 삼베의 역사는 오래지만, 무명은 14세기경부터 시작 되으리라 보고 있다. 즉 고려 말에 문

익점이 원나라에서 목화씨를 들여와 재배한 이후 함경도 일부를 제외하곤 한반도전역에서 재배되어 왔다. 무명 직조는 씨아로 목화의 씨를 빼고 물레로 실을 뽑으며 베틀로 짜는 과정을 거친다. 40자를 한 필로 하며 곱게 짠 것 일수록 상품(上品)으로 쳐서 그중 나주세목(羅州細木)이 유명하다. 관서(関西) 지방 에서는 담회색 혹은 담황색 무명배가 특산품이었다.

Cotton used to have an exchange value comparable to money. During the Yi dynasty the salaries of government officials were sometimes paid with cotton instead of money. Cotton was first introduced to Korea from China in the 14th century and since became the most widely used material for clothes.

To make cotton cloth first cotton was ginned and then yarn spun from the ginned cotton. The yarn then was fed into a loom for weaving. The finer the mesh of the woven cloth, the better the quality of the material.

⑮ 사　　찰(金蓮寺)
BUDDIST TEMPLE

184평(607.20M²)　조선시대　양식
184PYONG OR 607.20M²　STYLE OF YI DYNASTY

이 곳 사찰은 불교가 한국적토속화 (韓國的土俗化)로서 가장 한국적인불교의 모습으로 變化한 상태를 보여주는 사원이다.

주존(主尊)은 아미타여래(阿彌陀如來)이며 토속화의 신불(神佛)인 칠성 (七星)과 산신(山神)을 아울러 모셨다.

칠성은 각재(却炎)와 기자(祈子)자식 낳기를 비는 일) 및 산신(産神)의

상징이며, 산신(山神)은 산중(山中)의 모든 불신(佛神)과 중생(衆生),사물(事物)을 지켜주는 수호신이다. 이러한 신앙은 불교와 재래 한국의 민간신앙(民間信仰)이 습합(習合)한 토속적 신앙형태이다.

아미타여래는 서방극락정토(西方極樂淨土)를 주재하는 주불(主佛)로서 극락정토에 왕생(往生)하기를 원하는 민중의 내세(來世) 신앙을 상징한다.

이 아미타신앙은 신라이후 지금 까지 역사상 가장 광범위하게 민중의 신심을 이끌어온 한국불교의 대표되는 대중적 신앙이다.

The temple here displays the process in which Buddhism was transformed into a Korean version of the religion as a result of indigenization.

Enshrined here is the Amidabha as the principal image, accompanied by Ch'ilsong and Mountain God who are objects of worship among the Korean folk.

Ch'ilsong is worshipped as a god of fertility who is believed to be able to help women have sons and help families forestall disaster. The Mountain God is believed to be a guardian who is capable of safekeeping property for the masses. This indicates a mixture of Buddhism and the folk faith of the Korean people.

The Amidabha is the principal who governs the Paradise in the Paradise in the West.
He symbolized the people's faith in the future world and their wish to live in paradise after death.

The faith in Amidabha has led Korean Buddhists most widely through all the ages; hence, it can be regarded as representing Korean Buddhism.

관 아 (官衙)
PROVINCIAL GOVERNOR'S OFFICE

238.90평 (788.37M²)   조 선 시 대 양 식
238.90 P'YONG OR 788.37M²   STYLE OF YI DYNASTY

　지방행정을 담당하는 외관직 (外官職) 의 정무 (政務) 를 집행하는 곳을 관아 또는 공청 (公廳) 이라고 한다.

　지방행정의 단위 부서인 주, 군, 현, (州, 郡, 縣) 에는 각기 관찰사 (觀察使), 부사 (府使), 군수 (郡守), 현감 (縣監), 현령 (縣令) 등 지방장관이 있고 각종 공청이 있었다.

　여기 관아는 정문과 행랑 중문 (中門) 과 정청 (正廳) 인 동헌 (東軒) 과 내당 (內 堂) 그리고 내당 행랑등으로 구성되어 있고 후면에 옥사 (獄舍) 가 부설되어 있다. 한편 정문은 루문 (樓門) 인데 그 좌우로 연한 행랑은 상평청 (常平廳) 이다.

Office buildings for local government were called Kwana or Kongchong. Such units of local administration as Chu(district), Kun (county) and Hyon (prefecture) were headed by Kwanchalsa (governor), Pusa(mayor), Kunsu (county chief) or Hyonryong(prefectural magistrate).

One government building consisted of the main gate, outer servants' quarters on both sides of the gate, the inner gate, the main office(Tonghon) the magistrate's living quarters and the inner servants' quarters. At the back of the courtyard was a jail. The turreted main gate was flanked by servants' quarters and Sangp' yongch'ong.

동 헌(東軒)
MAIN OFFICE

가운데에 집무정청(執務正聽)이 대청으로 되고 그 양편에 큰 온돌방이 있다. 지방장관이 공사(公事)를 처리하던 공청(公聽)이며 장관은 예하 각 방관속(各房官屬)을 지휘하여 행정은 물론 사법까지도 통할 하였다.

flanked by lagre ondol (heated from below) rooms, the main floor (taechong) served as the main ottice space for the magistrate. The local administrative chief had jurisdiction over not only administrative affairs but also over judicial matters.

⑱ 남부지방민가

南部地方民家

HOUSE IN THE SOUTHERN PART

12평 (36.69M²)
12PYONG OR 36.69M²

19세기경 양식
STYLE OF 19th CENTURY

집단부락의 집들 가운데 비교적 고
격이 있는 민가형식의 하나이다. 규
모가 작은 편이며 방 2개와 광을 겸
한 넓은 부엌만을 갖춘 일자형 (一字
形) 집이다. 울산영병 (蔚山兵營)에는
과거에 많은 공방 (工房)이 있었으며
잡다하게 서민들이 모여 살았으므로
이집도 농사아닌 직종에 종사하던 사
람의 집이었다고 짐작된다.

This is the reproduction of a
19th century house as found in
Pyongyong, Ulsankun, Kyongsangnam-do. Among the houses of the
collective village of Pyongyong, this
is one of the oldest houses and
consequently somewhat antique.
Small in scale, it only has two rooms
and one kitchen which is used as a
store as well. In the past there
were many workshops in this district for the various artisans or
mechanics to work in. Perhaps
this house was one of those houses.

점복(占卜)

SHAMAN DEVINATION

점복은 인간의 앞날을 예언하여 그에 대처할 수 있는 준비를 하는 뜻에서 민간인의 지지를 받는다. 점복은 전문적인 수련을 쌓은 「점쟁이」(또는 점바치, 도사)에 의해서 이루어진다. 점복의 방법은 신통력에 의해서 하는 신점(神占)과 책력이나 성물(聖物)의 매체를 통해서 하는 두종류로 구분된다. 전자는 대체로 신이 내린 강신자 (降神者)들이 하고 후자는 학습 과정을 통해 숙련된 점술사(占術師)에 의해서 한다. 사람의 생(生), 시)時), 성명, 주소를 대면 점쟁이는 그 사람의 일년신수, 월수, 일수를 예언하고 그 대책을 지시해 준다. 점복의 종류는 「명두점」, 「신점」(神占), 「쌀점」, 「부채점」, 「산점」, 「굿점」, 「거북점」, 「씨점」등이 있다.

DEVINATION— People in the old days believed in devination because they thought knowing their future ahead of time would enable them to be ready for what was in store for them. The job of devination was carried out by trained professional fortunetellers. There were those who did this job by their occult power and those who told fortunes through the medium of a sacred physical object. A person visiting a fortuneteller was asked to tell the time, date and year of his birth as well as his name and address to have his future devinated by the professional man or woman.

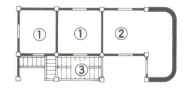

① 방(room)
② 부엌(kitcher)
③ 마루(wooden floor)

⑳ 남부지방민가 南部地方民家
FARMER'S HOUSE IN THE SOUTHERN PART

28.76평 (95.09M²)   **19세기경 양식**
28.76 PYONG OR 95.09M²   STYLE OF 19th CENTURY

일자형(一字型)을 기본으로 한 안채는 부엌에 딸린 부엌방을 약간 달아내서 변화를 보였으며 방사이에 큰 마루가 없이 두방이 밀착된 점이나 뒤쪽에 안사랑과 마루를 둔 점이 색다른 형식이다. 아랫채의 평면이 정4각형에 가까운 점도 특이한 점이다.

This is the reproduction of a 19th century farmer's house as fo-

und in Ipsokri, Yongkwangkun, Chollanam-do. Basically, the inner wing is a straight-line wing althought the kitchen is protruded at the back. It is unique not to have a wooden-floor room between the two rooms and to have a drawing-room and the wooden-floor room at the end. It is also unique that the plane of the outer wing is almost a square.

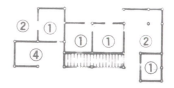

① 방(room)
② 부엌(kitchen)
③ 골방(back room)
④ 토방(earthera floor)

㉑ 중부지방민가 中部地方民家 FARMER'S HOUSE IN THE MIDLAND

41. 95평 (138. 70M²) | 19세기경 양식 8
41.95PYONG OR 138.70M² | STYLE OF 19th CENTURY

울안이 넓게 배치된 중부지방의 전형적인 ㄱ자형 농가형식이다. 문간체의 규모가 작고 바깥 사랑은 갖추지 못하였다. 건너방의 뒷방이 사랑방 구실을 하게 되며 대청에서 직접 부엌으로 드나들수 있게 된점이 특이하다.

This is the reproduction of a typical 19th century farmer's house with the shape of the letter '¬' as found in midland. It is noteworthy that the gate wing is very small in scale and that there is no drawing-room wing. In this case, the minor room of the inner wing functions as a drawing-room. It is also noteworthy that the kitchen can be reached from the hall itself.

① 방 (room)
② 부엌 (kitchen)
③ 대청 (wooden floor hall)
④ 광 (store room)
⑤ 헛간 (bara)
⑥ 외양간 (cowshed)

35

㉒ 중부지방반가 中部地方班家　대지 3,000평 건물 15동 275평　19세기경 양식
MIDLAND MANSION　　SITE 3,000 PYONG BUILDINGS (15 in all) 275 PYONG　STYLE OF 19th CENTURY

속칭 99칸집이라 부른다. 서기1861년 (고종12년) 수원성내에 지어졌던 것을 이건한 것이다.

솟을대문, 줄행랑, 바깥사랑, 안행랑, 안사랑, 내당, 초당, 내별당, 큰사랑, 외별당, 사당 등 유교사회에 있어서의 큰집 살림에 필요한 모든 공간이 규모 있게 갖추어진 전형적 대가 이다.

This is the reproduction of a 19th century mansion of 99kan or units as found in Suwon, Kyonggido. Fully equipped with all the accessories like the tall outer roofed gate, the haengrang or chain rooms on both sides of the gate for servants, the inner haengrang, the inner and outer drawingroom wings, a thatched cottage separated from the main or inner wing, the greater drawing-room wing, pyoldang or a separate building, a pond, and an arbour, this mansion built in 1861 belonged to a country gentlemen.

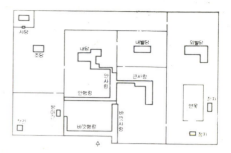

내 당
INNER WING
BUILDING

① 방 (room)
② 부엌 (kitchen)
③ 대청 (wooden floor hall)
④ 침방 (bed-room)
⑤ 골방 (back room)
⑥ 복도 (wooden-floor passage)

외별당
OUTER SEPARATE
BUILDING

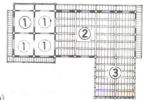

① 방 (room)
② 대청 (wooden-floor hall)
③ 누마루 (raised wooden floor)

큰 사 랑
GREATER DRAWING ROOM WING

큰 대청을 사이에 두고 큰방과 건너방이 있으며 큰방 아래는 복도를 통해지고 마루방과 달려 있으며 그 밑으로 상노가 대기하는 작은 온돌방이 한칸 달려있으며 큰방 후면으로는 내당으로 통하는 쪽마루와 복도가 부설되어 있다. 바깥 주인이 거쳐하는 사회적 공간이다.

The main hall is between the main and minor rooms. The floored passage attached to the main room leads to the book-stach, and next to the stach is the smallroom where a servant waits to be called. One raised floor-room is attached to the minor room. Behind the back wall of the main room are a small foor and a passage which leads to the inner wing. This wing is called a social space because it is here that the master of the house carry out all his social activities.

사 당 FAMILY SHRINE

옛날에는 살림이 넉넉하고 규모가 갖추어진 양반집안이면 집안에 사당을 모시었다. 위치는 일정치 않으나 후원 한편으로 규모가 큰 3칸집이나 간략한 단칸(一間)집을 짓는다. 대개 사대봉사(四代奉祀)하기 때문에 4 대에 걸친 양주신위(兩主神位)를 모시는 것이 상례이다.

Only a well-to-do family could afford to have a family shrine. It was customary to locate the shrine at the back. One's ancestors worshipped are one's parents, grandparents, great grand-parents, and great great-grand-parents. Ancestor-worshipping was the mainstay on which Yi dynasty's Confucian society stood.

안사랑 및 안행랑

INNER DRAWING-ROOM WING AND INNER HAENGRANG WING

48.56 평 (160.52M²)
48.56 PYONG OR 160.52M²

안사랑은 살림을 물려 준 노부모가 거처하기도 하고 자녀들이 쓰기도 한다.

안행랑은 유모, 침모, 찬모와 같은 여성들 전용의 거처공간이자 안심부름을 맡은 제한된 사람들이 출입하는 곳이기도 하다. 온돌 외에도 광이 부설되어 있어서 곡식, 기물 따위를 보관하거나 저장하기도 한다.

The inner drawing-room wing is either for the aged parents who have retired from active life or for the children. It also has rooms for the nurse, needlewoman, female cook, and maid-servant for the mistress of the house. There are four store-rooms for farm tools or produce.

안 초 당

INSIDE THATCHED COTTAGE

10.45 평 (34.56M²)
10.45 PYONG OR 34.56M²

혼전 따님들이 거처하거나 공부하는 공간이다. 내당후원 조용한 곳에 위치하며 규모가 작고 지붕에는 짚을 이었다. 조용하고 조촐한 면학(勉學) 분위기가 감도는 공간이다.

This is for the daughters to live in or to study in. Though small in scale, it is a very snug and beautiful thatched cottage.

㉕ 북부지방민가 北部地方民家
FARMER'S HOUSE IN THE NORTHERN PART

41. 33평(136. 62M²)   **19세기경 양식**
41. 33PYONG OR 136. 62M²   STYLE OF 19th CENTURY

관북지방의 꽤 큰 농가형식이며 공간의 배치가 매우 고르고 규모가 갖추어 진 집이다. 큰 부엌의 구들머리에 5개의 방들이 안마루 없이 밀집 양통(密集兩通)으로 구성되어 동절(冬節) 보온(保溫) 위주로 계획되어 있다. 규모가 큰 외양간과 방아간, 곳간도 정연하게 배치되어 있다.

This is the reproduction of a relatively very big 19th century farmer's house as found in Pukchong district, Hamkyongnam-do. Space is evenly distributed. The house is well contructed. It consists of a big kitchen and five rooms with twofold props. To secure and preserve maximum heat from the kitchen, the five rooms are back-to-back rooms without any wooden-floor room in between. It also has properly placed a cowshed, a mill, and a repository.

① 방 (room)
② 부엌 (kichen)
③ 광 (store-room)
④ 외양간 (cowshed)
⑤ 방아간 (Mill)
⑥ 제지공장 (paper mill)

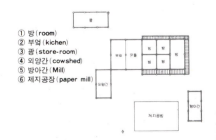

딱종이제조(韓紙製造)
MULBERRY PAPER MANUFACTURING

재래의 기법에 의한 닥종이의 제조과정은 대략 다음과 같다.

가을에 닥나무를 베어 큰 가마에 쪄서 껍질을 벗기고, 그 껍질을 물속에 하룻밤 재었다가 발로 밟아서 겉껍질을 벗겨 속껍질은 햇볕에 바래어 표백 백피(白皮)로 만든다. 백피(약간 누른 빛을 띤다)를 가마솥에 넣어 나뭇재로 내린 잿물을 섞어서 삶고 맑은물에 씻어낸 다음 씻어낸 백피를 이틀 밤낮동안 표백하고 방망이로 두들겨서 물에 씻으면 잿물이 빠지고 고운 섬유로 된다.

기틀(통)에 물을 채우고 섬유로 분해된 닥반죽을 푼다음 닥풀을 섞어 작대기로 휘저으면 곱고 묽은 반죽물이 되는데, 그것을 내빌(竹)로 물질해서 한장한장 떠내어 칸자리(紙台)에 엎어메고 통나무 궁글대를 굴려서 물을 뺀다. 3, 4백장으로 쌓이면 짐틀에 옮겨서 큰돌덩이로 지질러서 다시 물을 뺀다음 한장씩 메어 말린다.

It can be presumed that mulberry paper was produced as long ago as the Three Kingdoms period, the technique being transmitted from generation to generation. We still find being vestiges in some districts of the country. The conventional process of making mulberry paper is as follows:

Mulberry branches are cut in autumn and boiled in a large iron pot before bark is peeled off. The bark is soaked in water overnight. It is treaded on the outer skin of the bark peeled off. The inner substance is dried in the sun and made white through bleaching.

The white bark (a little brownish) is mixed with lye made of firewood ashes and boiled in water in an iron pot, then rinsed in clear water.

The rinsed bark is bleached for two days and nights. It is pounded with a mallet and washed in water to remove the lye. A large bucket is filled with water and the bark, now dissolved into fibre, is dissolved in the water. Mulberry paste is mixed with it. The whole thing is stirred with a stick to get a fine and thin gruel-like substance. The substance is scooped up, one layer after another, with a bamboo sieve and placed on a partitioned board. A long roller is rolled over it to squeeze the water out. Every pile of 300 to 400 sheets is removed to a frame and pressed with a large stone. After it is removed, every sheet of paper is dried separately.

㉖ 장터(市場) MARKET PLACE

우리나라의 장(場)은 신라시대에도 그 기록을 보일만큼 역사가 오랜 것이다.

특별한 시설을 갖추지 않은 일정한 장소에서 열리는 조선시대의 장은 15세기경 서울에서 먼저·형성되었는데, 화폐의 통용이 실시되면서부터 지방으로 확산하여, 전국의 1,000여곳에 장터가 생겼고 19세기말에는 1,600개에 달했다고 한다.

장은 1일 6일, 2일 7일등 오일장(五日場)으로 한달에 여섯번 개장된다. 이곳에서는 농민들의 농산물과 수공업자의 공산품이 교환되었고, 산간의 물산과 곡창지대의 곡물이, 해안과 내륙의 물산 등이 교역되었다. 한편 지방마다 장날이 엇갈리므로 장돌림 상품을 봇짐에 싸고 다니는 보부상(褓負商)도 교역의 큰 역할을 하였다. 이러한 교역 이외에도 새문물의 전파, 생활의 정보 교환에 이르기까지 장은 다양한 기능을 가졌다.

The history of market places in Korea goes back to the days of the Silla Kingdom. The more recent market places, simple open spaces where people from all parts of the country met with one another to trade their respective fares, however, were first opened in Seoul in the 15th century.

With the propagation of the use of the currency, the number of

the sites of market had increased all over the country to reach 1,600 by the end of the 19th century. Each designated site saw a market set up every five days for a total of six times a month.

At each market place the produce of the farming communities were traded with the artifacts produced by craftsmen, and the products of the interior with the riches from seaside communities. And since a market was set up on different sites on different days there were travelling businessmen who carried their fare on the back from a market site to another throughout the year. These travelling businessmen, pobusang, served as effective disseminators of new culture and imformation.

㉛ 물레방아(水車) WATER MILL

쏟아져 내리는 물줄기를 받아 그 힘으로 바퀴를 돌리고, 연결된 방앗대를 움직여서 곡식을 찧는 장치가 물레방아이며 그 집을 물레방앗간이라 한다. 이 방아는 바퀴에 물이 담기는 주머니가 연속으로 장치되어 있어서 주머니 물레방아라고도 부른다. 바퀴가 돌면 방앗대와 공이의 동작이 자동으로 되기 때문에 사람이 없이도 찧을 수 있다. 공이가 양쪽으로 두개 물려서 엇갈려 찧어지는 방아도 있고 한개만 있는 것도 있다. 주머니 물레방아외에도 물레 바퀴 아래로 흐르는 물의 힘으로 돌게된 물레방아도 있다.

The water power of a stream or brook was made to turn the wheels of this water mill. Attached to the wheels are a string of buckets which when filled with water pull and turn the wheels in one direction. This results in an up-and-down movement of a pestle linked to the turning movement of the wheels. The mill does not require the attendance of a man.

굴대와 방앗대
The part of the connection for the wheel mill

물레방아간 내부
The inside of the water wheel mill

㉜ 중부지방민가 中部地方民家

FARMER'S HOUSE IN THE MIDLAND

22. 21평 (73. 49M²)
22.21PYONG OR 73.49M²

19세기경　양식
STYLE OF 19th CENTURY

안채는 서울을 포함한 중부지방 특유의 ㄱ자형이다. 부엌안에 칸막이 하여 광을 둔 점은 특이하며 부엌에 연하여 안방이 2칸통으로 길게 연한 것은 특히 서울의 민가와 상통하는 형식이다. 외양간이 따로 있던 농가이다.

This is the reproduction of a 19th century farmer's house as found in Kakummyon, Chungwonkun, Chungchongbuk-do. The inner wing is typical of a '┐' shape wing as found in midland including Seoul. Somewhat uniquely. The kitchen is divided by means of a partition for a storing place. Next to the kitchen is the inner room with twofold props, as is the case with ordinary houses in Seoul. The cowshed stand separated from the inner wing.

① 방 (room)
② 부엌 (kitchen)
③ 대청 (wooden floor)
④ 광 (store)
⑤ 헛간 (bara)
⑥ 방아간 (mill)

엿

GLUTEN CANDY

우리나라 고유의 과자인 엿은 재료
에 따라서 찹쌀엿, 좁쌀엿, 수수엿,
감자엿, 고구마엿, 강냉이엿 등으로
나뉘어 지며 엿을 굳히기 직전에 섞
는 내용물에 따라서 호두엿, 잣엿, 호
콩엿, 깨엿, 호박엿, 생강엿, 계피엿,
같은 것으로 나눌 수도 있다.

엿은 다음과 같이 만들어 진다. 찹
쌀로서 고두밥을 찌고, 한편으로 날
보리를 싹을 틔운 엿기름을 빻아서 물
에 타서 채로 걸른다. 고두밥을 맑은
엿기름물과 뜨거운물로 잘 혼합시켜
서 독속에 넣고 당화시킨다. 당화가
끝난것을 삼베자루에 넣어 짜면 엿물
이 되는데 그것을 가마솥에 넣어 닳
도록 오래 끓이면 갱엿이 된다. 끝으
로 붉은 갱엿을 양쪽에서 당겨 바람
넣기를 하면 하얀 찹쌀엿이 만들어 진
다.

One of Korea's peculiar candies,
yot is classified into glutinous rice,
millet, sorghum, potato, sweet potato, and corn glutens by the material of which they are made and into
walnut, pinenut, peanut, sesame,
pumpkin, ginger, and cinnamon glutens by the seasoning which is
added immediately before the can-
dy is hardened.

Yot is made through the following process; Glutinous rice is steamed. Barley sprouts are pounded
into flour, which is mixed with
the
water and sieved. The steamed
rice is mixed with the watered
barley flour and hot water and

stored in a jar for saccharification.
The saccharified substance is put
into a hemp sack and squeezed to
get yotmul (watery gluten).
This is boiled in an iron pot for
a long time to get kaetyot (raw
gluten). The kaetyot, colored bark
brown, is stretched from both ends
like taffee until it turns white.

㉝ 제 주 민 가 濟州島民家
CHEJU HOUSE

30. 20평(99. 83M²)   **19세기경 양식**
30. 20PYONG OR 99. 83M²   STYLE OF 19th CENTURY

제주도는 남쪽으로 멀리 떨어진 섬으로 대양(大洋)의 거센 바람과 눈, 비가 많다. 이러한 자연 현상에 돌과 띠(茅)가 많은 조건이 결합되어 집은 낮고, 가옥의 3면벽을 돌벽으로 쌓게되었다. 지붕은 오래 견디는 띠로 이으며 띠로 다린 동아줄로 지붕을 총총히 얽어매는 독특한 가옥양식이 생기게 되었다. 그러나 제주도는 기후가 매우 따뜻한 곳이므로 육지에서 처럼 겨울철 추위에 대비한 채난, 온방(採暖, 溫房) 시설에 주력하지 않으며 따라서 부엌이라도 부뚜막을 두지 않고 솥을 따로 내걸어 취사하는 일이 보통이다. 따라서 가옥의 구조는 시원한 공간인 마루가 많은 편이며 개방적인 것이 특징이다.

This is the reproduction of a house as found in Cheju Island.

Being an island, Cheju has more rain and snow and wind then inland areas. It also has more stone and reed. These conditions of nature and resources make Cheju houses unique. Three walls out of four are made of stone and the roof is made of reed. The roof is tied up strong and tight with reed rope. On the other hand, the winter of Cheju Island is milder than that of inland areas. Their heating system is not a winter-oriented one. This accounts for the fact that they have more wooden-floor rooms in their houses.

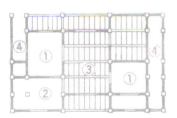

1) 방 (room)
2) 부엌 (kitchen)
3) 마루 (wooden-floor)
4) 헛간 (bara)

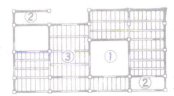

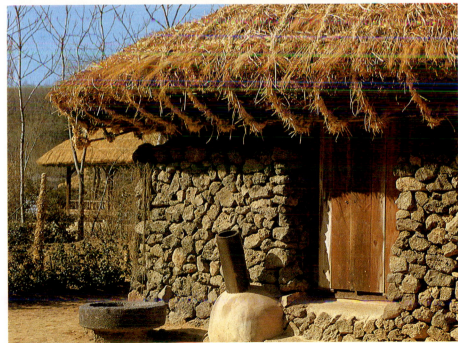

㉞ 남해연안민가 南海沿岸民家
SEASIDE HOUSE IN THE SOUTHERN PART

18. 56평 (61. 35M²)
18. 56PYONG OR 61. 35M²

19세기경 양식
STYLE OF 19th CENTURY

남부 해안지방에서 농업(農業)과 어업(漁業)을 겸업(兼業)으로 하던 민가의 형식이다. 몸체는 부엌이 양통형이다. 안방의 툇마루는 윗방사이와 후면으로 꺾여 돌았으므로 각방의 앞뒤에는 툇마루가 마련된 셈이다. 아랫채는 벽이 막돌담으로 축조되고 수장고와 온돌방, 외양간이 일자로 이어진 집이다.

This is the reproduction of a 19th century house as found in Koje area, Kyongsangnam-do. Koje being a seaside district, this is a house of a farmer and fisherman. The inner wing consists of the kitchen with twofold props, the inner room, the minor room, and a wooden-floor veranda between and around the rooms. The outer wing is made up with a barn of stone, a room, and cattle-shed.

① 방 (room)
② 부엌 (kichen)
③ 헛간 (bara)
④ 외양간 (cowshed)

㉟ 울 릉 도 민 가 欝陵島民家

ULLUNG ISLAND HOUSE

22. 44평(74. 06M²) **19세기경 양식**
22.44PYONG OR 74.06M² STYLE OF 19th CENTURY

부엌, 광, 곳간, 변소, 장독대가모 두 외벽으로 둘러 싸이고 사면 봉당 으로 공간이 연결된 일자형(一字形) 집이다. 겨울이 길고 비바람, 눈, 습 기가 많은 이 지역 기후조건에 알맞 게 이중외벽(二重外壁)을 치고 외벽 과 내벽사이에 봉당이 배치된 특수한 건축양식이다. 또한 이러한 구조는 부 엌에서 나온 연기가 봉당과 천정을 싸 감아서 천정위에 저장한 감자등의 곡

물의 방부효과와 방의 보온효과를 동 시에 얻을 수 있는 이점이 있다. 기 둥이 짧아 지붕이 낮으며 한집은 지 붕에 너와를 잇고 토벽을 쳤으며 한 집은 띠를 잇고 통나무 귀틀벽으로 꾸 몄는데 두집 모두 외벽에 이엉날개를 돌려매서 비바람을 막게 되어있다. 이 가옥은 울릉도에서도 고형(古形)에 속 하는 것으로 원형대로 옮겨진 것이다.

The kitchen, living room, storage room, toilet and the jar stand are all surrounded by an external wall. This linear house is connected by a dirt-floored space. This special architectural design features double-tiered walls for better heating effect in a way best suited to this area, which is subject to long winter, heavy snowfall, rainfall and wind. The structure aids in channeling smoke from the kitchen toward the ceiling and the dirt floor, thus better preserving farm corps such as potatoes stored in the attic from decay and maintaining the room temperature. Poles are short and the roof is low. One house is roofed with wood-blocks and has dirt walls, and the other is roofed with straw and has log walls. The straw wings tied to the exterior of the wall serve to prevent wind and rain from penetrating. They belong to an old type in the island community, and recreated true to the original shape.

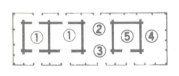

① 방 (room)
② 부엌 (kitchen)
③ 봉당 (corridor)
④ 변소 (toilet)

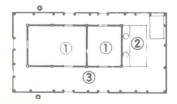

통방아
WATER MILL

물방아라고도 하며, 물레방아처럼 수력(水力)을 이용하여 방아를 움직여 곡식을 찧는 장치이다. 긴 통나무로 된 방앗대의 머리에는 직각으로 공이를 꽂고 뒷몸에는 구유와 같은 큰 물통을 파서 홈통으로 받아 내리는 물을 담게 되어있다. 이 물통에 물이 가득 채워지면 그 무게 때문에 물통이 기울면서 물이 쏟아진다. 이때 반대편의 앞머리 공이가 번쩍 들리고 동시에 물이 쏟아져내려 가벼워진 뒷몸이 위로 올라가므로 다시 앞머리의 공이가 확속으로 내리 꽂힌다. 이처럼 되풀이해서 확 속에 든 곡식을 찧게 되는데, 대개 하루종일 방아 스스로 동작하여 사람없이 곡식을 찧어낸다.

WATER MILL— Another type of water mill. A long thick log has a pastel fixed at one end and a hollow for receiving falling water at the other. When the hollow is filled with water its weight causes the pastel to rise. This in turn causes the hollow to spill its water content to make the pastel to fall and pound the grain in the mortar bowl. This process is constantly repeated with-out a man attending to the operation.

㊲ 연 경 서 원(研經書院)
YON GYONG SO WON

135평(445, 50M²)　조선시대 양식
135PYONG OR 445.50M²　STYLE OF YI DYNASTY

학덕(學德)이 높은 명현(名賢)을 제사하며 청소년들을 모아서 교육하고 인재를 양성하는 사설교육관이다. 우리 나라에서는 조선 중기부터 세워지기 시작했는데 1542년(중종37년) 풍기군수 주세붕(豊基郡守 周世鵬)이 순흥(順興)에서 고려의 학자 안 향(安向)을 모시는 사당을 짓고 백운동서원(白雲洞書院)이라 이름한 것이 최초의 서원이 되었다. 1550년(명종 5년) 퇴계, 이황(退溪 李滉)의 건의로 임금이 소수서원(紹修書院)이란 편액(編額)을 하사하니 또한 최초의 사액서원(賜額書院)이 되었고 서적과 노비, 전결(田結)이 사급(賜給)되었다.

한 때 쇠퇴해 가는 관설 교육기관인 향교(鄕校)를 대신하리만큼 그 수가 크게 증가했고 비중이 커지기도 했었으나 한편에는 그 폐단도 증가해서 이를 시정하는 방편으로 1865년(고종 2년) 전국에 47개 서원만을 남기고 모두 철회하기에 이르렀다.

서원의 외형적 구성은 명현의 위패를 모시며 제사하는 사(祠)와 차제를 교육하는 장소인 재(齋)가 기본이 되며 그밖에 서고(書庫), 판고(板庫), 비각(碑閣), 고직사(庫直舍) 등의 공간이 부설된다.

The sowon were private educational institute where memorial services for Confucian sages who were eminent in both learning and virtue were perfermed, and where able young men were taught. Sowon began to be established is great numbers in the middle part of the Yi dynasty period. In 1542 (37th year of King Chungjong), the magistrate of Pueggi County. Chu Sebung, built a shrine at Sunhung for An Hyang, a great Confucian of the Koyro kingdom, and named it Paegundong Sowon. This was the first sowon. Complying with a proposal by Yi Hwang (T'oegye). King Myongjong bestowed a nameplate in his own writing on Sosu Sowon in 1550 (5th year of his reign). This became the first sowon to which the royal gift of a name-plate was given. Soon another royal gift of books, bondmen, and fiefs followed.

The number of sowon increased so remarkably at one time that they could almost replace the function of hyanggyo, government-operated educational institutes, which were then on the wane. While the influence of sowon grew, they gave rise to a growing number of abuses. In order to rectify the situation, the government closed all but 47 sowon scattered throughout the country in 1865 (2nd year of King Kojong).

The sowon consisted of a sa where the tablets of noted Confucian sages were enshrined, before which they performed memorial rites, and a chae where they educated the youth. Other buildings were for book and woodblock storage, monume t houses, and dwellings for storage keepers.

다. 이들은 기예가 출중하여 광장에서
부락민들에게 「판굿」이라는 연회를 보
여준다. 농민들은 그들의 지신밟기와
같은 풍농제에서 뿐만 아니라, 벼를 심
은 논에서 잡초를 매는 김매기와 같은
집단 노동시에는 「두레풍장」이라는 농
악을 연주하여 그들의 작업능률을 높이
고 작업이 끝나면 「호미걸이」라는 농민
의 향연에 농악을 연주하며 군무(群舞)
로 즐긴다. 농악대는 크고 작은 여러
기(旗)의 기수(旗手)와 꽹과리, 장구,
징과 같은 타악기(打樂器), 악수(樂手)
와 호적, 나팔과 같은 관악기(管樂器)
잽이와 가면을 쓴 많은 무용수(舞踊手)
로 구성된다.

농악놀이 (農樂)
FARMER'S MUSIC-DANCE

　농민이나 어민들이 그들의 축제의식,
작업, 행진, 향연과 같은 때에 타악기
를 주로 하는 음악을 연주하면서 군무
(群舞)하며 많은 놀이를 연출하는 것을
농악(農樂)이라 부른다. 농촌에서의 풍
농제(豊農祭)와 어촌에서의 풍어제(豊
漁祭)는 농악을 연주하며 행하는 경우
가 많다. 농기(農旗)라 부르는 신간(神
竿)의 기능을 갖는 높은 기를 앞세우고
주민(住民)들이 악기를 연주하며 행진

하여, 부락을 지키는 신(神)을 모신 당
산(堂山)에 올라가 제(祭)를 지내고,
신을 모시어 부락의 여러집을 행진하며
풍농 풍어를 축원해 준다. 끝에는 부락
민들이 넓은 광장에서 농악을 치며 군
무(群舞)로 향연(享宴)을 베푼다. 부락
주민이 아닌, 걸립패 또는 굿중패라고
일컬어지는 유랑의 농악대가 있어, 지
역마다 차례로 방문하여 돈을 받고 축
제의식(祝祭儀式)을 베풀어 주기도 한

Music-and-dance was an ever
present feature of farming and
fishing villages. The event would
start with a procession of farmers
or fishermen playing various tradi-
tonal musical instruments visiting
the village shrine to pay homage
to the community's guardian gods.
The procession then moves on to
make a tour of all the houses of
the village to drive away evil
spirits and usher in good fortune.
The finale of the event was a group
dance performed at the village
gathering ground. When the music-
and-dance ritual was performed at
places of work, paddies and farms,
it provided a rhythm of labor.
A farmers' music-and-dance procession was led by flag bearers
included players of percussion,
wind instruments and dancers.

널뛰기 SEESAWING

널뛰기는 부녀자의 야외오락 (野外娛樂)의 하나로서 음력 정초와 오월 단오, 팔월추석등 큰 명절에 주로 성행되었다. 12자(尺)정도의 길이의 두꺼운 널판 한 가운데 밑을 짚묶음 또는 가마니 뭉치로 벼개를 만들어 괴고, 널판 양끝 위에 한 사람씩 올라서서 교대로 뛴다. 뛰었다 내리는 반동으로 두사람의 몸은 점점 공중으로 높이 솟아 오른다. 널뛰기는 고려시대부터 전래된 오락으로 여겨지며, 속설(俗説)에 의하면 옥에 갇힌 남편을 보기 위하여 담장밖에서 두 여자가 널뛰기를 처음 시작 하였다고 한다.

Seesawing was one of the favorite outdoor games of women played on such major traditional holidays as the lunar New Year day, "Tan-o" (the fifth day of the fifth lunar month) and the August Moon (the 15th day of the eighth lunar month). A thick wooden-board of about 12 feet in length was used as the seesaw. Straw bags were folded and piled one upon the other under the wooden board half-way between both ends of the board to serve as an arbor.

Two persons standing on the board, at both ends jump up and down alternately. The up-and-down motions of the two players give an ever increasing impact on their ends of the board as they are flung increasingly higher in the air. According to folklore the origin of the game goes as for back as the Koryo dynasty when two women are said to have brought a seesaw to outside the window of a jail where their husbands were inmates to steal a glimps of their beloved from the height the sea-saw sent them up.

㊵ 중 부 지 방 농 가 中部地方民家
FARMER'S HOUSE IN THE MIDLAND

24. 08평 (79. 47M²)
24. 08 PYONG OR 79. 47M²

19세기경 양식
STYLE OF 10th CENTURY

중부지방에서는 일반형이 아닌 일자형이면서 양통형에 가까운 가옥 형식이다.

부엌머리의 안방다음에 있을 대청이 앞면으로 쏠리고 안방 옆으로 두개의 방이 맞붙어 세개의 방이 밀집되어 있다. 마루는 대청에 툇마루의 중간적 형식이다.

This is the reproduction of a 19th century farmer's house as found in Kongju, Chungchongnam-do. Its structure is irregular for a midland farmer's house because the rooms are with twofold props and because the rooms are back-to-back rooms. Also irregular is the wooden-floor veranda, which is, in fact, a compromise between a hall and a veranda.

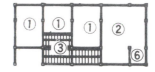

① 방 (room)
② 부엌 (kitchen)
③ 대청 (wooden-floor hall)
④ 광 (store room)
⑤ 헛간 (bara)
⑥ 방아간 (mill)

㊶ 남부지방민가
南部地方民家
FARMER'S HOUSE IN THE SOUTHERN PART

23. 29평 (70. 33M²)
23. 29PYONG OR 70.33M²

19세기경 양식
STYLE OF 19th CENTURY

남부 특유의 일자형(一字形) 집 두 채를 ㄱ자형으로 배치한 형식이다. 안채는 한가운데에 마루 한칸이 있고 그에 연해 두개의 온돌방이 있어 규모에 변화가 있으며 아랫채에도 양쪽에 두개의 마루방이 있어 수장공간의 규모가 증가했음을 보여준다.

This is the reproduction of a typical 19th century farmer's house in Wolsong, Kyongsangbuk-do, having two straight-line wings positioned like the letter 'ㄱ'. The wooden-floor room in the very centre of the inner wing can be said to be a variation upon the otherwise normal structure. The drawing-room wing has two wooden-floor rooms at the extrems right and left respectively. The existence of the two wooden-floor rooms means the enlarged space for storing farm produces.

① 방 (room)
② 부엌 (kichen)
③ 마루 (wooden-floor)

㊷ 남부지방민가 南部地方民家
FARMER'S HOUSE IN THE SOUTHERN PART

27.03 평 (89.38M²)
27.03 PYONG OR 89.38M²

19 세기경　양식
STYLE OF 19th CENTURY

남부지방 소농가의 일반형인 일자형집 2 채를 ㄱ자형으로 배치한 형식이다. 아랫채는 안채의 좌향 축에서 약간 벗어난 배치를 보인다. 안채의 마루방은 온돌방보다 축소 되었으며 건너방 앞으로 별도의 부엌이 마련된 것은 일자형(一字形)의 변형이다.

This is the reproduction of a 19th century small farmer's house as found in the southern part. It consists of two straightline wings positioned in the shape of the letter ' ㄱ '. The wooden-floor room of the inner wing is smaller than the rooms with the under-floor heating system. To have another kitchen in front of the minor room is a variation on the straight-line wing.

④ 중부지방민가 中部地方民家 　34.55 평 (114.03 M²) 　19세기경 양식
FARMER'S HOUSE IN THE MIDLAND
34.55PYONG OR 114.03M² 　STYLE OF 19th CENTURY

　중부지방 민가의 일반형인 일종의 튼口자형 가옥 형식이다. 부엌과 일자(一字)로 안방이 마련된 것은 경기지방과도 공통되는 형식이다. 안 대청과 사랑마루 툇마루가 고루 갖추어져 있다. 대문간은 안벽이 차벽으로 되어 있어 안밖격식(내외관념)을 염두에 두었음을 알 수 있다.

This is the reproduction of a

19th century farmer's house as found in Kongju, Chungchongnam-do. As is the case with other 19th century midland farmer's houses, the lay-out of this one modelled itself upon the letter '口' with open corners. That the kitchen and the inner room are positioned on the same straight line is what this house has in common with its counterpart in Kyonggi-do. This house has

the inner wooden-floor hall and one wooden-floor veranda. There is a screen-wall behind the main entrance which prevents the inner wing from being seen by strangers at the gate.

㊹ 남부지방대가 南部地方大家

70. 31평 (232. 03M²)   19세기경 양식

BIG HOUSE IN THE SOUTHERN PART

70.31PYONG OR 232.03M²   STYLE OF 19th CENTURY

ㄱ자모양의 안채와 일자형인 사랑
채, 광채가 튼 □자형으로 배열된 형
식이다. 방과 마루의 전체 공간배정
이 서로 비슷한 마루가 많은 대가이
다. 안뜰과 사랑뜰이 각각 넓게 잡히
고 대문 밖에도 넓은 마당이 있는 규
모가 큰 남부 토반집의 표본이다.

This is the reproduction of a
19th century big house as found

in Yochon, Chollanam-do. The
inner wing shaped like the letter
'ㄱ', the drawing-room wing, and
the store wing are positioned like
the letter 'ㅁ' with three open corners. There are a lot of wooden-
floor rooms as big as rooms. Beside
all this, the house has one spacious
quadrangle and one large backyard.
This is an example of a country
gentlemen's largescale house.

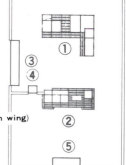
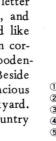
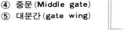

① 안체 (inner wing)
② 사랑체 (drawing-room wing)
③ 광체 (store wing)
④ 중문 (Middle gate)
⑤ 대문간 (gate wing)

안채
INNER WING

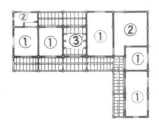

① 방 (room)
② 부엌 (kitchen)
③ 대청 (wooden floor hall)
④ 골방 (back room)

사랑채
DRAWING ROOM WING

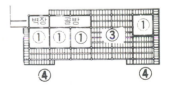

① 방 (room)
② 부엌 (kitchen)
③ 마루 (wooden-floor)
④ 누마루 (raised wooden-floor)

㊼ 남부지방민가 南部地方民家
FARMER'S HOUSE IN THE SOUTHERN PART

18. 90평 (62. 40M²)
18. 90 PYONG OR 62.40M²

19세기경 양식
STYLE OF 19th CENTURY

　　두채의 일자형(一字形) 집을 ㄱ자
로 배치한 남부지방 일반적인 소농가
형식이다. 안채의 마루방은 툇마루로
대치되었고 넓은 부엌머리에 작은 부
엌방이 달린 것도 한 특색이다. 외양
간과 광으로 겸용되는 공간이 윗방머
리에 달린 것도 색다른 점이다.

Positioned in the shape of the
letter 'ㄱ' this reproduction with

two wings represents small 19th
century farmer's houses in the southern part.　The floor room is
replaced by a floored veranda.
What makes this house unique is
the built-in room at a corner of the
kitchen. Another peculiarity is the
addition to the right-hand side room
which functioned as a cowshed and
a store-room as well.

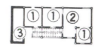

① 방 (room)
② 부엌 (kitchen)
③ 광 (store-room)
④ 변소 (toilet)
⑤ 헛간 (bara)
⑥ 돼지우리 (pigpen)

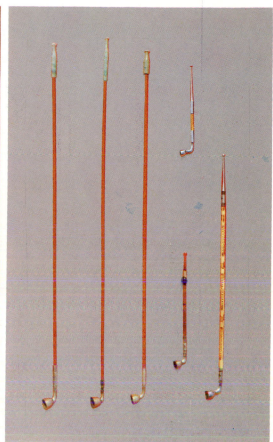

담뱃대공방 TOBACOO PIPE MAKER WORK SHOP

한국에 담배가 전해진것은 17세기 이후이며 담뱃대는 이때에 만들어 졌으리라고 생각한다.

경남 동래가 원산지이며 현재는 울산, 김천, 남원등지에 전승되고 있다.

담뱃대는 흡연구(빨뿌리), 중간대(살대), 담배를 담는 (꼬불대)로 구성되고 재료는 구리, 백동(白銅), 수정(水晶), 자기(磁器)등으로 만들어진다.

The bowl and mouthpiece of the traditional long-stemmed tobacco pipe were made of copper, alloy of copper and tin, crystal or porcelain. Those of the best quality were ones made of the copper-tin alloy inlaid with blackened copper and silver for decoration. The production process involved heating, forging and soldering.

㊽ 중부지방민가 中部地方民家
FARMER'S HOUSE IN THE MIDLAND

18. 15평 (59. 98M²)   **19세기경 양식**
18. 15PYONG OR 59. 98M²   STYLE OF 19th CENTURY

두채의 작은 일자형 집을 ㄱ자로 배치한 소농가형식이다. 안채는 마루가 없이 넓은 부엌과 방앞 퇴칸의 토방이 연속되는 극히 간소한 형식을 보인다.

윗방 머리에 작은 광이 달린 것이라던가 부엌안에 찬간을 칸막이 한 것 등은 그런대로 최소한의 기능적 구성을 보인다.

This is the reproduction of a 19th century farmer's house as found in Kongju, Chungchongnam-do. This small farmer's house consists of two wings which are positioned like the shape of the letter 'ㄱ', Humble in structure, the inner wing has no wooden floors but only a kitchen, two rooms, and a small erathen-floor veranda. Having a pantry and a small store-room, however, it is eqipped with minimum functional facilities.

① 방 (room)
② 부엌 (kichen)
③ 찬간 (pantry)
④ 광 (store-room)

㊾ 중부지방민가 中部地方民家
FARMER'S HOUSE IN THE MIDLAND

27. 77평 (91. 68M²)
27.77PYONG OR 91.68M²

19세기경 양식
STYLE OF 19th CENTURY

안채는 남부지방 일반형인 일자형의 직은 집이며 아래 윗방에 뒷마루가 붙어있는 간략한 형식이다. 사랑채는 두개의 큰방과 외양간, 헛간이 있는 양통(겹) 집이다. 안밖이 모두 중부지방 농가로서는 특이한 구성을 보이는 예이다.

This is the reproduction of a 19th century farmer's house as found in Asan, Chungchongnam-do. Having a straightline shape, the inner wing represents a typical style of farmer's houses in the southern part of Korea. It has a simple structure, consisting of two rooms and a wooden-floor veranda. The outer wing which have twofold props, consists of two big rooms, one cowshed, and one barn. This house is unique in style and composit on for a midland farmer's house.

① 방 (room)
② 부엌 (kitchen)
③ 토방 (eatther a floor)
④ 외양간 (cowshed)
⑤ 헛간 (bara)

㊿ 대장간 (冶匠間)
BLACK SMITH'S
WORK SHOP

단철(대장간) : 시우쇠를 단련해 철기 (鐵器)를 만드는 장소를 대장간이라 하고 거기서 일하는 기술자를 대장(冶匠), 야장이라 한다. 대장이란 본래 야장의 우두머리를 가리키는 말이다. 무쇠는 녹기 쉬워 주조가 가능하나 무쇠보다 탄소(炭素) 함유량이 적은 시우쇠(鍛鐵)는 불에 달궈 두드려 기물을 만든다. 한국에서 철의 역사는 약 2천 5백년 전으로 소급된다. 근래에 재래식 주철소(鑄鐵所)는 볼수 없게 되었으나 대장간만은 지방곳곳에 그대로 남아 있어서 농기구와 연장(工具) 및 그밖의 생활 도구등을 제작하거나 부속품을 공급해 주고 있다. 시우쇠를 단련하는 일 가운데 최고의 기술은 도검(刀劍) 제작이다. 이는 일반적인 시우쇠에 동철(봉씨)로 날 빼기를 해서 단조하는데, 당금질에도 고도의 기술을 필요로 하는 것이다.

The traditional blacksmith's shop where heated pig iron was beaten into ironware was called Taechangkan and the crafts-men working there Taechang while iron was easily molten and cast into products, pig iron withless carbonic content than iron had to be heated and forged. The history of iron-making in Korean goes back to some 2,500 years ago but the traditional method of iron-making has largely disappeared from the scene. There are, however still, an occasional Taechangkan seen operating in some rural villages to produce farming instruments and other implements of living by the taditional method.

The hardware that required the most sophisticated skill to produce were swords and knives. These weapons of the olden days were made by the traditional tempering method.

농기구전시장(農機具展示場)
SHOW ROOM FOR FARMING TOOLS

유기공방
BRASSWARE SHOP

유기(鍮器)라 하면 놋쇠로 만든 기물(器物)을 통칭한다. 그러나 그속엔 구리 합금의 두 종류가 있다. 그 하나는 구리와 아연(亞鉛) 합금의 주동(鑄銅)이 있고, 구리와 주석합금의 유동(鍮銅)이 있다.

주동은 진유(眞鍮)라고도 하는데, 이는 쇠물로 주조해 물건을 만들며, 아연의 독때문에 식기로는 쓰이지 못한다. 유동은 쇳덩이를 불에 달구어 두드려서 물건을 만든다. 방짜는 놋쇠의 최상품으로서 유동을 말하며 통쇠는 최하품 주동으로서 이른바 잡동(雜銅)이다. 방짜는 찰흙의 야밤에만 작업한다. 어둠 속에서 쇠의 열도를 가늠하며 수명의 대장(冶匠)이 매칠 해 기물을 만든다. 징, 꽹과리, 바라같은 악기를 비롯하여 온갖 녹식기와 대야, 요강 백호칼에 이르기까지 모두 방짜 제품이다. 현재 이 같은 제품은 김천(金泉), 함양(咸陽)등지에서만 생산되고 있다.

There are two types of brassware. One is made of an alloy of copper and zinc, the other of copper and tin. The former cannot be made into tableware because of the toxic substance of zinc. Unlike the copper and zinc alloy which is made into cast goods in motley form, the second alloy is heated and then forged into products. This forging process is carried out in dark where the craftsmen are able to discern the degree of heat of the metal by the light emanated by it. Items made by this process includes cymbals, gongs, tableware, basins, chamber pots, etc. The history of iron in Korea goes back to 2,500 years ago, though it is no clear by what process people made iron. The traditional methods of making farming tools and other implements of living with iron, however, can be seen today at blacksmith's shops which are still a regular feature of rural communities across the country.

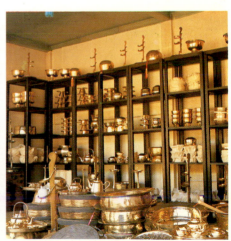

값 2,000원

印刷 1985年　6月　11日
發行 1985年　6月　16日

編 者　朝元觀光振興株式會社
　　　　韓　國　民　俗　村
發行者　圖書出版　文　　園
　　　　金　允　淑
서울特別市 江南區 驛三洞 706-18
電話 : 556-1867
印　刷　民 俗 企 劃 文 化 社
　　　　陳　　駘

登錄番號 80. 1. 23. 第 1-384號(複製不許)
잘못된 책은 교환해 드립니다.